LET'S GO TEAM:
Cheer, Dance, March

LET'S GO TEAM:
Cheer, Dance, March

MARCHING BAND
Competition

Judy Garty

Mason Crest Publishers
Philadelphia

Mason Crest Publishers, Inc.
370 Reed Road
Broomall, PA 19008
(866) MCP-BOOK (toll free)
www.masoncrest.com

First printing

1 2 3 4 5 6 7 8 9 10

Library of Congress Cataloging-in-Publication Data

Garty, Judy.
  Marching band competition / Judy Garty.
     v. cm. — (Let's go team—cheer, dance, march)
Includes index.
Contents: The prize — The history — Behind the scenes — The show —
The champs.
  ISBN 1-59084-539-0
  1. Marching bands—Competitions—Juvenile literature. [1. Marching
bands—Competitions.] I. Title. II. Series.
  MT733.4 .G37 2003
  784.8'3143—dc21

                                                                    2002015959

Produced by
Choptank Syndicate and Chestnut Productions
226 South Washington Street
Easton, Maryland 21601

Project Editors Norman Macht and Mary Hull
Design Lisa Hochstein
Picture Research Mary Hull

Printed and bound in the Hashemite Kingdom of Jordan

OPPOSITE TITLE PAGE

Although contest criteria vary, marching bands typically earn points for general effect, visual effect, and music. Judges may also evaluate a band's brass and percussion sections, ensemble music, and color guard.

Table of Contents

SLINGER HIGH SCHOOL
MARCHING BAND
SLINGER, WI
WISCONSIN
1848

The Prize

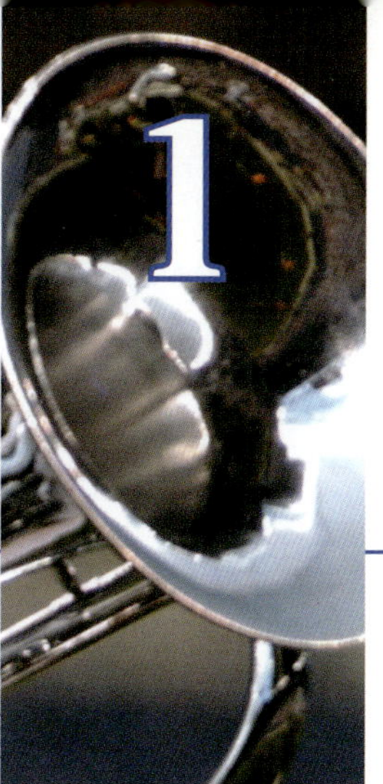

Ten minutes before the end of the last school day before Christmas break, December 22, 2000, Slinger High School's 26-year band director David Hanke got a phone call that changed lives. Interrupted by a fire drill, he only had three minutes left in the school day to call the office secretary and ask her to make an announcement. What came over the public address system sent students into the hallways screaming, jumping, and hugging each other. The Slinger High School Marching Band from the village of Slinger, whose population was barely over 3,000, had been chosen to represent the state of Wisconsin at the January 20, 2001, Inaugural Parade in Washington, D.C.

The Slinger High School Marching Band was one of only 21 high school marching bands chosen to participate in the Bush Inaugural celebration.

The Slinger band was one of only 21 high school bands in the country chosen for the Inaugural Parade honor. Invited by a state senator to enter the competition, they submitted an audio tape with a dozen of their songs and a 12-minute videotape of their performance. After the tape passed a military screening, it was sent to the Inaugural Committee. The committee reviewed an unknown number of applicants and informed Hanke that Slinger was one of the top two Wisconsin choices. Though the band had hoped to learn the final choice of the President-elect's Inaugural Committee in early November, election delays pushed that decision into late December.

The band would be leaving January 17, and the news spread like wildfire. Parents were alerted and asked to come to a meeting for details. The 130-member band needed money to travel to Washington, D.C.; transportation; a place to stay; and chaperones. Expenses were estimated at $90,000, which would have to be raised quickly. Since the marching band season had ended weeks earlier, the band uniforms would need to be unpacked and re-packed for travel. Marching routines would have to be rehearsed. Forget winter vacation; there was work to be done.

Band boosters sprang into action. More than 200 people worked on committees to help the marching band. One parent, who did not even have a student in the band program, volunteered as the fundraising chairperson. She made phone calls to companies and organizations she thought might be willing to send money to the band. One band grandmother donated a large, stuffed Winnie the

Slinger High School Marching Band members wave enthusi-astically as they begin their journey to Washington, D.C.

Pooh to the band to be raffled for money. A band dad painted "Go Slinger Band Go" in the snow where the band would see it. Other parents helped with sweatshirt orders, sold marching band buttons, signed up to travel with the band, got school cell phones for the chaperones, and arranged to post a trip diary of words and photographs on the band's Web site for the families back home.

Slinger, Wisconsin was behind the band all the way. In 1997, the community had contributed $70,000 to buy the band new uniforms. They had also supported fundraisers for a band trip to Disneyland. Now money for the parade was pouring in. Local media tallied the daily totals.

Donations came from a rival high school, the local grocery, the American Legion and Auxiliary, many area businesses and individuals, and the state's football team, the Green Bay Packers. Over 850 groups and individuals from all over the state sent money. By January 4, they had $46,000 toward their needed total of $90,000. Three days later, the donations totaled $63,000. At the end of two weeks, they exceeded their goal and raised $106,000.

Band director David Hanke and his assistant, Steven Zenz, scrambled to make arrangements. They spent hundreds of hours getting ready for the event. Wisconsin Governor Tommy Thompson—the President Elect's choice for the Health and Human Services post in Washington—even helped the band by making sure they got the best price for their train tickets.

A WINNING AUDITION

Lovell Ives, Director of Halftime Activities for the Green Bay Packers since 1982, reviews marching band itineraries and videos every year looking for the three or four he will invite during the August to December season. "They have to be strong musically and with a big sound, a driving percussion section," says Ives. "The marching has to be precise. The format of the show has to be entertaining, more than marching. You can't stand still—there has to be a lot of action and movement on the field." Each halftime show lasts 6.5 minutes, and the sound has to be big enough to fill the stadium of nearly 70,000 spectators.

During Christmas vacation, the high school marchers practiced their individual music at home and practiced marching together—inside the school building, outside on the streets by the school, past houses in the neighborhood, and around the parking lots of nearby stores. Whenever people heard them, they came out to clap and cheer. When school started again, the marching band practiced every day before lunch. Even in light snow, they rehearsed outside. The students called their upcoming trip a once in a lifetime opportunity. For many, it was the highlight of years of practice.

The band was featured on television and in the local newspapers. By departure day, they were ready. After an auditorium send-off, the banner bearers, rifle squad, color guard, and band musicians boarded five buses and were escorted through town to the highway by a loud stream of police cars, fire trucks, and rescue trucks. Six staff members and 43 chaperones traveled with them; other parents would join them in Washington, D.C. In Milwaukee, they filled two double-decker train cars and spilled over into two other units. Their band instruments, uniforms, and luggage traveled by truck. The band ate in half-hour shifts and coped with time zone changes. Their 21-hour train trip sent them through seven states.

The Slinger High School band was met at Union Station in Washington, D.C., by a state senator, a police officer, and a Wisconsin television crew. After checking in at their hotel, eating dinner, and doing some sightseeing, they slept. At 8:30 the next rainy morning, they were rehearsing "Patriots on Parade" and "On Wisconsin"

The Slinger High Marching Band marches in the 54th Inaugural Parade on January 20, 2001. The parade was so large it had four divisions and over 10,900 participants.

in a parking garage. Later they performed at a reception for Governor Thompson at Union Station. In between practices, they visited some of Washington's historical sites. Saturday morning they went to the Pentagon where they were security checked. The weathermen were calling for rain with possible sleet or snow. The band brought hand and foot warmers, ear headbands, insulated under-wear, special glove warmers, and grain alcohol spray to keep their instruments from freezing. They were bused to the mall area at 11 A.M., in parade position by 1 P.M., and scheduled to march at 4 P.M. Nearby were warming tents with hot chocolate and clam chowder. But once the band was in parade position, they were unable to use the tents. A cheering group of parents and family met them en route. They were the fifth group to march in the fourth division of a parade with over 10,900 participants. They stood tall at 12th and Pennsylvania as they marched before the 43rd President of the United States, George W. Bush. None of them will ever forget the moment when they paraded past the President's reviewing stand and he waved at them.

"It was a huge event and a very big deal," said Hanke. "The bands that get chosen are bands that have poise, that know how to carry themselves. You've just got to be 100 percent there. You have to have confidence—it comes from practice and learning to do things exactly the right way. It stems from desire, commitment, and pride. We try to pay attention to all the details."

The Slinger band toured Washington before they left and posed for a group photo in front of the U.S. Supreme Court building. They visited the Smithsonian, enjoyed a dinner cruise on the Potomac River, viewed the Vietnam War Memorial, and watched their band directors lay a wreath at the Tomb of the Unknown Soldier at Arlington Cemetery. From Senator Herb Kohl's office, they accepted a flag flown over the Capitol on the day of the 54th Inaugural celebration. Despite some sniffles, a few flu bugs, and lots of tired bodies, the marching band members each had an important souvenir—the pride they felt in playing for the President of the United States.

The History

Marching bands go back to ancient times. They have roots in military and religious ceremonies, in pageants, and in entertainment. In many cultures, martial (military) music inspired men into battle, signaled advances and retreats, bolstered soldiers' spirits, and celebrated their bravery.

Marching bands use a combination of brass, percussion, and woodwind instruments, which have to be carried as they march. Marching band instruments include flutes and piccolos, French horns, saxophones, clarinets, trumpets, trombones, tubas, drums, cymbals, and triangles. Some bands add the glockenspiel, an

Some of the marching band instruments have been around for thousands of years, but their sound quality has changed over time. The modern trumpet, for example, can play a greater range of notes than its ancient forebears.

instrument resembling a xylophone, to their percussion section. There are also marching bagpipe bands.

PERCUSSION INSTRUMENTS

Ancient Mesopotamian artwork from 4,000 B.C. depicts kettle drums. Percussion instruments like cymbals were used by the ancient Egyptians, Assyrians, Greeks, Romans, and Hebrews. The handheld tympani, or tambourine, is an example of a percussion instrument that has not changed much over time. Traditionally made from skins and shells, it is the same for people who use it today, like the Canadian Ojibwa and Cree First Nations, as it was for the ancient Middle Eastern people with whom it originated. African slaves introduced xylophones to Latino communities during the Spanish conquest in the 16th and 17th centuries. Drums and castanets accompanied ancient Roman dances. The triangle originated with Turkish Janizary music, which combines triangles with cymbals and different sized drums.

BRASS INSTRUMENTS

Brass instruments have some unusual ancestors. The Etruscan cornu, or war horn, was 126 x 55 inches, making it much too big for today's marching bands. Still it was an important army instrument for its time and was also played at gladiator fights. The Etruscans also used the lituus, which looked and sounded like a tuba.

Horns date to 2,000 B.C. First used as a hunting horn, the French horn was made in France in the mid-1600s. Its 12 feet of coiled tubing could produce about 12 notes, the

Percussion instruments like the drums have been used by many cultures all over the world.

natural harmonic series. By the 1750s, musicians began putting a hand in the bell, adding more notes. Valves were added in the 19th century. The first trombones, or "sackbuts," as they were once called, date to the 14th century. By the 1500s there were three sizes of trombones: alto, tenor, and bass. Near the end of the 18th century, the trombone's narrow bell became a widely flared bell.

Trumpets, first made in ancient times from conch shells, were later made from silver and bronze by the

Egyptians, who added long, straight tubes and flared bells. Two trumpets were found in the tomb of Tutankhamen, an Egyptian pharaoh, or king.

Over time, improvements have changed the way instruments are made and how they sound. For example, the Bluehmel piston valve, invented in the 1820s, made it possible for brass instruments to play lower notes. This piston valve led to the invention of the chromatic trumpet, the s-shaped trumpet we know today. Unlike the modern trumpet, ancient trumpets were straight and could play only the natural tones.

COURAGE UNDER FIRE

During World War I, each company of the Canadian Expeditionary Force was accompanied by a bagpiper. The pipers volunteered to lead the charge from the trenches, and their death rate was high. A 20-year-old Scottish-born electrician from Vancouver named James Richardson was the piper for the 16th Battalion when they fought the Germans in northwest France on October 9, 1916. When the Canadians came to a barbed-wire barricade, Piper Richardson ignored the gunfire and grenades and played marches, strathspeys, jigs, and reels to inspire the men to advance. Richardson survived that attack, but later fell to another. Never found, Richardson was presumed dead. After his death, he was awarded the Victoria Cross—the highest British and Canadian military decoration—for his bravery in playing the bagpipes. He was the only Canadian piper ever to earn this honor.

The tuba's ancestors include the lituus and the bucina, ancient brass instruments that were played in the military and at competitions, processions, and funerals.

The modern tuba was patented in 1835 by Prussian bandmaster Friedrich Wilhelm Wieprecht and German builder Johann Gottfried Moritz. The marching band tuba is usually the baritone tuba, also called the euphonium, or the three valve sousaphone. The marching bugle tuba is common in drum and bugle corps.

WIND INSTRUMENTS

Flutes began as ancient twin-reed flutes, or panpipes, named for the Greek muse Pan. Over time they became one-piece instruments with six finger holes. During the 1600s flutes were built in three sections with connecting joints. By 1800 the flute had four keys and then eight. Beginning in 1832, Theobald Boehm of Bavaria perfected a ring-key system for cylindrical flutes that used at least 13 tone holes and padded keys. Modern flutes are based on Boehm's model.

The fife is a high-pitched member of the flute family. It has a single bore, six tone holes, and no keys. The piccolo is a high-pitched type of transverse flute, originally made of wood.

Early clarinets had many shapes before the 17th century, when the model used today was perfected. Native Americans had a short tube with two hollowed-out cedar wood pieces and a tied reed. The South American version used a gourd, and the African bumpa was played like a flute. Snake charmers played a kind of clarinet, and double clarinets could be found in South America and Europe.

Belgian instrument maker Adolphe Sax invented the saxophone around 1840. There are three saxophones: baritone, tenor, and alto.

BAGPIPES

Bagpipe music started with the MacCrimmon family. Around 1670 they opened a bagpipe school at Borreraig on the Isle of Skye. The college offered a seven-year course of study and existed for over 100 years.

The ancient Greeks had bagpipes, and the ancient Roman bagpipe is still used in Italy today. The traditional Scottish bagpiper held a place of honor in wars before the 18th century. Bagpipe bands were still used in the military as late as 1918, when Canada sent about 30 pipe bands to World War I.

MARCHING BAND MUSIC

Until the 1600s, military musicians learned their music by copying one another. In the 17th century, composers began writing music especially for marching bands. Jean Baptiste Lully, a French composer and musician, was the first composer to write out drum parts. As time went on, more and more composers wrote marching music for bands, including Johann Sebastian Bach, Johann Christian Bach, and Wolfgang Amadeus Mozart. By the age of 29, Franz Joseph Haydn was writing marches for military groups. C.P.E. Bach wrote several outdoor sonatas, and Michael Haydn wrote a Turkish band march. Hector Berlioz wrote the first book on orchestration. He also wrote music for brass bands with as many as 108 band members.

MARCHING BANDS IN NORTH AMERICA

Scottish fur traders, explorers, and adventurers brought pipe bands and the bagpipe to Canada about 200 years ago. Early American Puritans and Quakers did not allow bands, but the Germans, Dutch, and Swedes brought music with them when they emigrated to North America. George Washington, who wrote about a parade at Valley Forge, had a military band of fifes and drums, and the British had several military bands in America. One of the first well-known American band leaders was Josiah Flagg of Boston. By 1773 he was holding concerts in Boston with up to 50 musicians.

The Massachusetts Band of Boston, formed in 1783, had ties to the Massachusetts Volunteer Militia. The American Band of Providence, Rhode Island, was a civilian marching band. The United States Marine Corps Band began in 1798. The United States Military Academy Band began in 1815. By the 1850s, professional military bands were playing at the graduations of colleges like Harvard and Princeton.

During the American Civil War, there was at least one drum and bugle band at every major battle. At the Battle of Gettysburg, there were ten bands. At the end of a fighting day, the Union and Confederate armies would have a musical battle of the bands.

John Philip Sousa became conductor of the U.S. Marine Band in 1880. He toured the world and was called the March King. He wrote 136 marches, and they were so popular, they are still part of many parades today.

SCHOOL BANDS

The first official uniformed college band began with 11 members at the University of Wisconsin in the 1880s. Albert Austin Harding was band director at the University of Illinois from 1907 to 1948. His motto was "Always something new." Over the years, the University of Illinois band, known as the Marching Illini, had several firsts. It

The University of Wisconsin band, organized in the 1880s, was the first official uniformed college marching band.

was the first college band to use field bugles, mallets, and sousaphones; the first band to have its own band building; the first school to have a symbolic mascot; and the first college band to post a Web site and release a compact disc. The Purdue All-American Marching Band, which began in 1886, was the first to stage a night half-time show with the musicians wearing tiny, battery-operated strings of lights. In the 1960s, the Cal Band of Berkeley, California, which grew out of the 1891

University Cadet Band, began using flash powder to announce its field entrance. This fireworks-type explosive created a flash of brilliant light, a cloud of smoke, and a "whoosh" sound that made the band's appearance dramatic and spectacular.

From the time school marching bands began to play at football games, they were visible ambassadors of school spirit. Athletic games, pep rallies, and homecoming parades depended more and more on the marching band to enliven them and get people on their feet clapping and cheering for the home team. Color guard, which has its roots in the military, grew beyond carrying the flag and rifles to carrying school colors, sabers, and decorative swing flags. This auxiliary part of the band led parades and added sparkle to the band on the field. Marching bands developed more and more ways to entertain and involve the audience and to showcase their music and marching maneuvers.

Field formations started in the early 1900s when the Marching Illini formed the school letter, a block "I," in a parade and later, using a section of students sitting in the bleachers with cards, at the football stadium. In the late 1930s, University of Wisconsin band director Raymond Dvorak came up with formations without signals. One formation was an airplane and another spelled out the post-game score. In the 1960s the Cal Band developed a pre-game formation in which the marchers took the shape of a flying wedge. When this band played "America the Beautiful," the marchers spread across the entire football field to write "Cal" in script. Military and symmetrical

Marching bands began using field formations in the early 1900s, often spelling out school letters. Here the University of California Marching Band, or Cal Band, forms the letter "C" on the field.

field formations kept expanding to include choreographed routines with original, free form drills.

MARCHING BAND UNIFORMS

Traditionally, military bandsmen wore uniforms decorated with lace and braid to contrast with the uniforms of the regular troops. Since commanders wanted to know where their signal men were at all times, their drummers wore uniforms that were easy to see. As school bands

Color guards add another exciting visual effect to marching bands through the use of props such as decorative swing flags.

became more popular, marching band members wore school colors. Today, band uniforms often include pants, suspenders, a jacket, and gloves. Helmets with chin straps and plumes are sometimes worn. Shoes are sometimes covered with spats, which protect them from mud.

The tartan, a plaid textile of Scottish origin, is part of the piper uniform. Piper bands can trace the history of their tartans. The Galt Kiltie Band of Cambridge, Ontario, Canada, for instance, began in 1902 and took its first green, blue, and black check tartan from a 1739 regiment that guarded against cattle raids.

One of the first known marching band contests was planned by Prussian military bandleader Wilhelm Wieprecht. Wieprecht organized a band day in 1838, conducting 32 bands and 1,200 musicians for the entertainment of visiting dignitaries.

Around 1923, band contests and festivals began. By the 1960s, marching bands were popular and the number of band competitions grew. In the 1970s, symmetrical drill patterns were popular. Baton twirlers and swing flags were often part of the show, and American bands often presented the U.S. flag in their routines. Percussion players tended to be on the 50 yard line with the banner line in the backfield.

By the 1980s, color guards and percussion lines took a bigger part in the show. The marching was fast-paced, and the color guard routines were more demanding. There were fewer baton corps, pom lines, and swing flags. The music, too, was more difficult, ranging from classical pieces by composers like Dvorak and Stravinsky to popular music and show tunes.

The 1990s saw flashier uniforms and more daring color guard drills. The marching was more demanding and the music more varied. Marching tunes could be as different as *Phantom of the Opera*, Beatles' songs, or music from *Titanic* and *God Bless the Child*. Today's performances are limited only by a band's imagination.

Behind the Scenes

Marching bands are an entertaining and colorful example of school spirit or community pride. Whether playing at football games or representing their school or group away from home, bands are meant to be watched and heard for pleasure. Marching bands are mood setters. Their music indicates whether the listeners should be standing to salute a flag or shouting to cheer on a team.

Marching band takes time. Members need time to master their music and make sure they coordinate their playing. Learning steps and routines takes time and practice. George Parks, who gives marching band leadership workshops across the United States, says, "Practice

The marching band, led by a drum major, always sets the mood for the occasion.

makes permanent." So it is important to pay attention to details during practice times.

In middle school and high school, band time goes beyond the school day. For those who participate in extra-curricular bands, members have to save some free time for rehearsals, performances, and travel. There can be the individual music lesson time, sectional practice time, group marching time, and independent practice time. Some school bands rehearse before or after school, and some practice at night, on weekends, or during summer vacation. Band members with special duties, like drum majors or band librarians, have to put in extra time for many different tasks.

Luther Appel, Band Director at Bay Port High School in Green Bay, Wisconsin, was Director of the Regina Lions Band in Saskatchewan, Canada, for 12 years. His community band was really four bands with marchers from age 7 to 19 who progressed from one band to the next. According to Appel, Canadian and American marching bands are organized much the same and are more popular in some areas of each country than others. American bands perform in both fall and summer, while Canadian bands are more active in the summer. He recalled one time when his band did a run-through on a field that had four inches of snow, and they had to shovel the sidelines.

Appel says, "It takes tons and tons of time and work to put together a competitive marching band. You can teach everybody to be a good marcher. If they're dedicated to it, that makes the difference."

Forming a competitive band is a group effort. Besides the bandleader, there are many other workers who help keep the band running smoothly. In a school, the principal has to support flexible scheduling and be willing to allow band rehearsals. School board members must support a band director's requests for equipment, guest musicians, and travel that will improve the music program and the quality of the band.

Parents and volunteers have a major support role in any band program. There will be times when chaperones are needed for events or trips, and volunteers fill that need. Sometimes volunteers make phone calls or help with sweatshirt or t-shirt orders. Some band directors are lucky to have volunteers who are handy with a needle and thread; they can help with minor uniform repairs.

Community bands also depend on the support of others. Many times groups like the Lions Club will sponsor a community band. The club gives the band a place to rehearse and helps pay for band directors and supplies.

BAND CAMP

Many colleges offer band camps in the summer months. Participants pay fees to cover their meals, housing, and instruction. Sometimes discounts and scholarships are available. There are special camps for drum majors and section leaders, color guard, and marching percussion. Bands of America (BOA) holds summer band camps for over 60,000 participants and 200,000 spectators each year.

BAND DIRECTORS

Band directors are key players in any marching band. They set the goals and motivate the marchers to achieve them. The band director and assistant director are partners. The assistant should be able to take over for the director at any time. The director must be a musician and teacher.

Before the season begins, the director will make plans, review music, and perhaps find ideas for shows. With the help of a band staff, the director can begin copying and arranging music for the upcoming season. Each new school year, the music library and music folders are cleaned and ordered; uniforms and school instruments are cleaned; new members are measured for uniforms.

At a summer band camp, the director can drill the band as a group for the first time, teaching the group how to line up, step together, and master their charts. The charts have diagrams showing drill formations for field marching. The director might hold auditions to help place the right people in the right parts of the band.

As the season progresses, the director will help the band members refine their routines, motivate them, communicate any important information to the field announcer, and make sure the marchers know how to enter and leave the field.

DRUM MAJORS

A drum major helps the band director during rehearsals. Sometimes drum majors wear earphones or carry walkie talkies so they can be in direct contact with

The drum major leads the band onto the field and sets an example for the other band members to follow. He or she may use a baton to conduct the band, making sure everyone is following the routine and working together.

the band director even if they are far apart from each other. During a show, drum majors are the conductors; the band director is not on the field. The drum major's main job is to keep the marching band members on task and working together. They set the pace for rehearsal drills by using hand, voice, whistle, or baton signals. They help members learn the routines and discuss any problems with the director. The drum majors have to be used to the music and ready to conduct on the field and at rehearsal.

SECTION LEADERS

Marching bands have section leaders in charge of groups of instruments. In a large band, there can be a section leader for each group of instruments. Sometimes section leaders will set up special group rehearsal times. The section leader, also called a rank sergeant, often communicates messages to and from the band director, and contacts section members when needed.

LIBRARIAN

The band librarian works closely with the directors to take care of the music. New music has to be stamped, processed, and copied for the musicians. All music must be stored and catalogued. Field folders need to include

TRAINING FOR A MILITARY BAND

The Armed Forces School of Music at Little Creek Amphibious Naval Base in Norfolk, Virginia, trains musicians for the United States Marine Corps, Army, and Navy. Training lasts six months. After the music school, Marines are assigned to one of the 12 Marine Bands in the world. There are nine Navy Bands, 12 Air Force Bands, over 30 Army Bands, and three Military Academy Bands. U.S. Army bands entertained over 27 million people around the world in 2001.

There are presently 23 pipe bands for the Reserve Forces of Canada and 11 pipe bands for the Regular Force units in Canada and Germany.

the right musical pieces in the correct order. Worn or torn music may need repair or replacement. At certain times of the season, music has to be given to the musicians or collected from them. The librarian makes sure that exchange runs smoothly. The librarian tells the band director where the files are, what pieces may need updating or replacing, and whether more copies are needed.

EQUIPMENT MANAGER

In some bands, there is a separate equipment manager; in others, the individual section leaders monitor the equipment. Whoever is in charge of equipment has to keep records about the instruments, uniforms, and all equipment except the music. The equipment manager might help set up chairs and stands before rehearsals or help load and move equipment for travel. This person helps issue and collect equipment, making notes about anything that needs cleaning or repair.

BUSINESS AND PUBLICITY MANAGERS

Whether or not there are separate people to do these jobs depends on the size of the band. Sometimes these tasks are done by the director. Whoever is handling the business has to keep records, make phone calls, keep track of band money, and direct fundraising. The publicity manager is in charge of letting people know what the band is doing. This could mean calling TV or radio stations, newspapers, magazines, or community organizations. The publicity manager might get volunteers to make and distribute posters for marching band events.

The Show

Building a band takes time and patience. As the band loses its older members and gains new members, adjustments have to be made. Because a marching band works as a group, it can be compared to a family. Every person in the band has a responsibility to help one another and to do a fair share of the work. A winning show routine does not happen overnight.

Larger competitive bands often have a professional write their show for them. Smaller bands without the same kind of money in their budget usually leave the routine writing to the band director. No matter who writes the show, each routine should suit the band performing it.

Show band style marching, the most dramatic of the march styles, is physically demanding as band members must keep a high-stepping pace.

The marchers should enjoy the challenge of performing it well. Practice is the key. Somewhere along the way, the marchers will know they are ready. Then it is time to go out and compete.

CLASSES OF MARCHING BANDS

Contest criteria vary widely from state to state and province to province. School size and the number of people in the band help decide a band's class of competition. Different classes of bands can compete in the same events. A band might petition its state organization to go up or down a class in order to compete with similar quality bands.

No matter what class a band belongs to, it can use any of three styles of marching: military, corps, or show band. Military is the traditional style of marching and uses a crisp walking step. Corps style marching is similar to traditional military marching but uses a roll step. Show band style, or high-stepping marching, is used by some of the large university and college marching bands to set them apart from other bands.

Marching bands usually use the same style of marching as drum corps, brass and percussion bands that perform in parades and competitions. Marching band and drum corps competitions also use similar judging criteria. Bands are given points for general effect, visual effect, and music. These contests also evaluate the band's brass, percussion, ensemble music, and color guard.

TYPES OF COMPETITIONS

There are three kinds of marching band competitions: audition, rated, and sweepstakes. Sometimes marching bands prepare a show with the energy and dedication of a competition, but perform simply for the enjoyment of entertaining the public—like the Dunvegan Girls' Pipe Band of Westville, Nova Scotia, Canada. Other bands live to compete and can be in contests every weekend of the season. Some drum corps groups travel thousands of miles over the summer and compete in tens of competitions.

Schools can hold invitational competitions. Run like high school athletic contests, state music organizations can sanction several regional shows through which bands can qualify for divisional contests and state or provincial championships. Championship competition can be fierce, with scores separated by only hundredths of points. Groups like Drum Corps International also hold national and international competitions.

No matter what type of contest a marching band enters, the band will be judged on how well it performs, how well the group mastered its music and steps, and what originality and imagination the band put into its show. The maneuvers don't have to be difficult, but they have to be as perfect as they can be.

SWEEPSTAKES COMPETITIONS

Sweepstakes competitions are the most common kind of marching band contest. There are more field show sweepstakes than parade sweepstakes. This competition awards places to each band, and most bands want to be number one. That goal gives a band a reason to do its best, but rivalries can develop between competing bands. In this kind of contest, there will be winners and losers, so participants have to be ready to deal with different emotions. The judging format depends on the contest. The grading system can add up points like the system used for rated contests or it can be the kind that starts with 100 points and deducts points for mistakes.

RATED COMPETITION

In a rated contest, which can be a field show or a parade, each band is judged on how well it performs its routine. This judging is similar to the kind used in the solo and ensemble competitions of concert bands and musicians. There is no overall winner, and the band does not know how it compares to other bands. Each band starts out with a clean slate and builds up points for every detail the judges score. Bands receive divisional ratings like First Division (also called Superior), and Second Division (also called Excellent). One band does not influence another band.

This kind of contest is a good way for beginning bands to start competing. It gives them the experience of a contest but takes away the pressure of trying to beat another band. Depending on the contest sponsor, rules can differ; but the main points rated bands are judged on are their musical performance, marching fundamentals, special drills, and special effects.

AUDITION COMPETITION

The audition kind of contest is different from the field show and parade competitions. The preparation is the same, but each participating band does not know or see the other bands. In an audition, competing bands submit their audio and videotapes and then wait to hear from the judges. A band can audition to be in a parade like the Tournament of Roses or in a field show like the halftime show for an NFL Packers football game.

PARADE MARCHING

Bands who march in parades may have won an audition to be there, or they may be competing in a rated or a sweepstakes competition. Sometimes bands travel a great distance to participate. While there are some parade

Since the 1960s the Cal Band has used flash powder, a fire-works-type explosive device that creates a cloud of smoke, to announce its entrance to the field.

competitions with only marching bands, it is more common to have marching band parade competitions as part of a parade where there are also floats, clowns, and fire trucks. Because of the short time a parade marching band will be in front of the judges' stand, bands sometimes measure how far it is from the start of the parade to that stand. That way, they can plan the best part of their routine to happen right in front of the judges.

FIELD SHOWS

Bands who give field shows may have won an audition to do so, or they may be competing in a rated or a sweep-stakes competition. Sometimes bands travel a great distance to be there. Unless weather forces this contest indoors, marching band competitions take place on football fields. Entrants sign up and pay fees to participate. Each show has specific rules, and the band should be aware of those rules ahead of time. The band can lose points, for instance, for going over the time limit. Certain music or maneuvers might be required.

JUDGING CRITERIA

Judges are called adjudicators, and they are in demand. The National Judges Association (NJA), which provides judges for the Tournament of Bands (TOB), assigns about 2,500 judges each year. Judging systems also vary. The Illinois Band Festival, held for all senior high school bands in Illinois, uses an Olympic scoring system. Bands are scored by five judges, the high and low scores are removed, and the three middle scores are averaged.

A judging panel looks for very specific things. A timing judge strictly monitors time. He will signal the band to start and warn them when time is almost up. A cadence judge has to watch that the band is marching with the correct number of beats per minute. The cadence judge might check the marching step by watching a metronome. An individual bandsman field judge checks band members for posture, instrument handling, playing, and marching. A general field judge checks for how the group is lining up and spacing themselves. An overall field judge watches to see how smoothly the band moves in and out of its maneuvers. The musical judge listens to the sound and makes comments about how the musicians articulate and blend. An instrumentation judge checks to see if the band has the right number and ratio of instruments. Finally, an inspection judge is looking for neat uniforms and polished instruments.

The Tournament of Bands (TOB), a competitive organization with 400 active member schools in nine states, has a 100-point scoring system. Judges are looking for straight lines, clear cut turns, good spacing, and uniform starts, stops, and halts. They want the music to have

WHAT IS DRUM CORPS?

Drum corps today is a competitive marching band composed of brass and percussion instruments as well as color guard. Drum corps has a long and varied history. Connecticut's Mattatuck Drum Band began in 1767 and has had members for over 230 years. John Phillip Sousa wrote an instruction manual for drum and bugle corps in 1886. The Drum Corps Hall of Fame was founded in 1966. The Boston Crusaders gave the late President John F. Kennedy an honorary membership, and they were the first drum corps to carry double bass drums horizontally. The Blue Devils were the first drum corps to win every caption at Drum Corps International (DCI) Finals. The Royal Crusaders set a world record on April 16, 1978, for constant drum playing on a 20-mile march. In 1979 the Phantom Regiment had a Baskin-Robbins ice cream named after it to help promote the DCI Northern Championship in Ypsilanti, Michigan. The New York Lancers Corps appeared on *Sesame Street* to explain rhythm.

clear attacks and releases, good rhythm, coordinated beat, good tone, and precision in each section. They look for a variety of visual effects and a performance that blends well with the music. Judges look for inventive drills and original ideas that make the audience feel something. TOB can also give specialty awards for percussion, color guard, drum major, brass, and woodwinds. Penalties are given for talking, being over or under time, and for not having heels together.

The Wisconsin School Music Association (WSMA) uses a panel of eight judges to grade field marching events. The panel sits in a press box overlooking the football field. Participating bands have signed up before the deadline and paid a minimal fee to participate. The judges have a checklist to help them score each band. Unless the weather is poor and the contest has to be moved indoors, the competitions are held outdoors. The judges can watch as many as 30 or 32 bands in a day. Each band presents an eight to eleven minute show, and there are 15 minute intervals between groups. What each judge is scoring is very specific.

Before the competition, the judges spend time studying the contest criteria. They have to rate each band in a particular category against a certain number of points. The total number of points adds up to 100. The judges not only score each band individually, but they rank the bands against each other. Part of their job will be to make an audiotape of their comments for each band director. Each band director will have five minutes in a critique session at the end of the contest to talk with the judges and hear their comments and advice. Because there are eight judges, each band director will receive eight tapes.

There are execution judges that examine how well the band is doing its job. One judge rates the band on its music execution. This judge is paying attention to the sound of the band and watching to see how well the musicians play alone and together. Another judge is rating the band's visual execution, looking closely for straight lines, uniform curves, exact spacing, and how well each band member is marching. These two categories are each worth 20 points.

Another set of judges are the general effect judges. This is a more artistic category and can be harder to judge; in Wisconsin there are two judges for each of the general effect categories. The number of points the band receives in these categories will be an average of the two judges' scores. Dan Petersen, former master adjudicator for WSMA and the Central States Judges' Association (CSJA), is band director at Longfellow Middle School in Wauwatosa, Wisconsin. Petersen says, "The easiest way to describe general effect is to call it the goosebump quotient. There's an energy in a performance, and that's what they're judging."

The music general effect judges pay special attention to the difficulty of the music, how well the music is written, how well the musical drill uses the field, and the overall presentation. The two visual general effect judges look at how the costumes match the program, how creative the formations are, and how the band displays their showmanship and spontaneity.

Drum corps combine a marching brass and percussion band with a color guard to create an exciting and beautiful performance.

There are also judges for the categories of percussion and auxiliary. The percussion judge watches the battery percussion—the snare drums and quads—and the front line percussion or the pit—the timpani, xylophone, and electronic instruments. The auxiliary judge rates the band's color guard on how well they add to the show. The highest WSMA score in each of these two categories is 10 points.

The Mid-States Band Association (MSBA) covers high school marching bands in Ohio. Their competitions use a regulation football field marked every five yards. The competition field includes a zone between the 35 yard lines, five yards deep, with markers at the four corners and fifty yard end lines. MSBA requires at least five judges: three to judge general effect up to a total of 60 points, and two to judge music and visual performance for a 40-point total. There can be optional judges, and no judges are allowed on the field. Three of the judges have to be assigned by the MSBA, and the head judge must be one of those three. The bands' 15 minute intervals include their set-up and warm-up, and timing penalties are awarded in tenths of points. Judging starts with the first march step or note of music, and bands can exit the field with rim taps or a percussion cadence.

COLOR GUARDS ADD TO THE SHOW

Color guards are often at center stage during a marching band performance, and the music is in the background. Color guards use props that go along with the music and the theme of the show. They toss flags, run, roll, jump, spin, and do splits. Sabers, decorative rifles, flags, and batons are among their props. Their costumes add glitter to the show.

PIPE BAND COMPETITION

The judging criteria for pipe bands are a little different. Rules of the Eastern United States Pipe Band Association (EUSPBA), for instance, tell how many pipers, snares, and bass drums make up each of five grades and give the age range of each level. In general, pipers are judged on their musical introduction, tempo, breaks, finishes, tuning, execution, expression, and the tone of their chanters and drones. Drums are scored on their rolls, tone, tempo, execution, blend, rhythm and expression, quality, and variety. The ensemble or group performance is judged on technique, sound quality, how uniformly the group played together, the quality of the arrangement, and musicality.

APPEARANCE

The clothes band members wear should suit their show. If the routine is military, the costumes and actions of the band should be military. If the routine has a tropical flavor, Hawaiian shirts might be used. Sometimes marchers even change clothes during a competition. Unless there is a particular reason to dress some band members differently from others, everyone should be dressed the same. The standard uniform should be clean, and it should fit properly. The cap should be sitting on the head properly. Uniform buttons should be buttoned. Usually the boys are asked to be clean shaven and the girls are asked not to wear jewelry.

Besides how they look one by one, the marchers have a group look as they move around and perform. The days of just standing still and playing songs are past. Alan Rick Temby, a drill designer from Indiana, has been writing marching band routines since 1978. He writes about 23 shows a year for high schools and colleges in Illinois, Ohio, Mississippi, North Carolina, and Wisconsin. According to Temby, Indiana bands are very competitive and use about 60 different charts for one marching band show.

There are many different ways band members can move on a field. Whichever band instruments and musicians have the featured parts should be visible and easy to hear. Sometimes the horns might take center stage and the drill will move past and around them. A show will have movements to link its opener, color presentation, concert, out of concert, and closer.

Competitors have only six to eleven minutes to present a theme or tell a story. Temby and other designers work to put the music with the moves. They look at how many musicians play each instrument, whether the color guard will be changing equipment during the show, and what tempo each piece of music is. "If you show a lot of enthusiasm," said Temby, "it makes a big difference. It contributes to the overall believability of the show."

SOUND

A marching band show needs enough music to fill its time. A show that runs about seven minutes will commonly use at least three or four different songs. The variety of those songs and how they blend together is important. The music is a big part of the band's overall presentation. The instruments will play, what they are supposed to play–melody or counter-melody, harmony or rhythm. Whichever music part is meant to be heard the most should be closest to the audience and easiest to hear. Since different instruments are featured at different times, movements in the routine should feature the right musicians at the right time.

One show might start with a loud and attention-grabbing opening number to attract the audience. That could be followed by a slow, ballad-type song with the auxiliary units waving their flags to the music. The closer could be another up-tempo tune. Sometimes a band will feature soloists or an ensemble. Bands might add a choir to their show or feature the pit—the electronic keyboard, marimbas and timpani—as the front line. Sometimes the looks and sounds make perfect sense and are what the audience expects; other times there is a surprise look or sound that will grab the audience's attention in a new way.

The show is where all the practicing, all the talent, and all the elements come together. It is holding the saber at just the right angle and changing flags at just the right time. It is hitting the notes precisely on time and stepping together just as you have rehearsed. In only a few minutes, the band will introduce themselves to the audience and leave them with a memory of who they are and what they did together in the show. Everything the band has been rehearsing is on display at the show. How well each group performs in their few minutes decides the winners.

The Champs

Marching band champions stand tall. They enjoy what they do. They know their music and their drill, and it shows. The best bands have an extra energy, a sparkle that seems to say, "Look at us! We're having fun!" It is easy to see which bands have practiced and are having fun on the field or in the parade. How do you get to be a champion? Practice, practice, practice. But if you love the music and the marching, you will enjoy the fun of working together to make something special.

There are many contests available for marching bands. Large organizations hold competitions every year. Some contests are held in the same place every year, others

It takes practice to build a good marching band, but for those band members willing to devote a lot of effort to their craft, the rewards are numerous.

Marching band members learn good sportsmanship by acting as ambassadors of good will and representing their schools or communities wherever they go.

move their location. The Saskatchewan Music Festival began in 1908. It now represents 230 community music festivals with 250,000 Canadians of all ages playing everything from piano to steel drums. Bands of America (BOA), founded in 1975, has 60,000 teen participants each year with 230,000 audience viewers. The Traditional

Youth Marching Bands Association (TYMBA) was formed in 1983. Tournament of Bands (TOB), founded in 1972, has over 400 active schools in nine states. No matter where you live, there is a school or organization near you that can get you marching in a contest. Show bands, drum corps, pipe bands, and traditional marching bands all have competitions.

Planning a contest is a lot of work. The organization or school that will host the competition has to make sure it has a large enough space for the marchers and the audience. Changing facilities, bathrooms, and parking space will be needed. A competition costs money, and the organizers will have to decide what fees to charge. Fundraising is one way to raise money for expenses. Once the space is found and reserved and the fees are set, information about the event must reach the bands that might be interested in competing. Publicity volunteers can use the Internet, telephone, newspaper or magazine ads, and letters or postcards to publicize the event.

If bands will be coming from far away, people will want to know about places in the area where they can stay, eat, and maybe visit. Organizers will have to line up judges and awards. Many times group photographs, event videos, and souvenirs like t-shirts are offered to competing bands and their fans. Volunteers will be needed to make and post signs and help with registering bands, answering questions, helping people know where things are, and sometimes running scores from the judges to the posting area. Whatever people might need—first aid, food, water, telephone service, emergency instrument repairs—will have to be provided.

Most of the rules for being part of a competition are common sense. Participants should come prepared and be on their best behavior. Just like you, the other bands are there because they enjoy music and marching and they are hoping to perform well. It is appropriate to clap and cheer at the end of a group's performance. It is not appropriate to boo or to distract members of another group. Knowing how to be a good winner or a good loser is part of good sportsmanship. Participants at the event are representing their schools or communities and are expected to be good role models. Anything you say about other bands should be positive.

Dave Matthys, Band Director at Cleveland High School in Portland, Oregon, has 22 years of experience with marching bands. A marching band adjudicator for the Northwest Marching Band Association, he said, "Never let the judges' score(s) dictate how you feel about the show you perform. If you did your best and you feel good about how you performed, that is much more important than the score you receive."

Videotapes and audiotapes of performances can be helpful. Before or after competitions, band members can watch and hear their routines to see if there are any parts they need to work on. Watching other bands in competition is another way to learn what looks and sounds good.

Winning a championship is a thrill and an honor. There are many ways excellence is rewarded. Some marching band competition winners take home a trophy or a cash

WINNING THE SUDLER TROPHY

The Sudler Trophy for Excellence in College Marching Bands is the top college marching band honor in the United States. This national trophy is presented by the John Philip Sousa Foundation. It can be won only once, and it is awarded to the college or university marching band that has demonstrated a history of high musical standards, innovative marching routines and ideas, and important contributions to the advancement of college marching bands. Past winners include:

2002 – Louisiana State University

2001 – Texas A&M University

2000 – University of Georgia

1999 – Texas Tech University

1998 – University of Massachusetts

1997 – West Virginia University

1996 – University of Nebraska

1995 – Purdue University

1994 – James Madison University

1993 – University of California at Los Angeles

1992 – Northwestern University

1991 – Arizona State University

1990 – University of Iowa

1989 – Kansas University

1988 – Michigan State University

1987 – University of Oklahoma

1986 – University of Texas at Austin

1985 – Florida A&M University

1984 – Ohio State University

1983 – University of Illinois

1982 – University of Michigan

A drum corps performs on the field at the 2002 DCI Drums Along the Rockies event in Denver, Colorado. Many bands travel long distances to compete.

prize for their school. Ribbons may be individually awarded to the top band members. In audition-type competitions, the reward is being named to participate in a special event like the Presidential Inaugural Parade or to travel as goodwill ambassadors. A record of good marching may lead to a band camp or college scholarship.

The Burlington Teen Tour Band of Burlington, Ontario, Canada, has 185 members, boys and girls, ages 13 to 21. Rob Bennett, who began playing in the band 26 years ago, is managing director. According to Bennett, what the band does for the young people goes beyond awards and honors. "It's an organization for youth to grow and become productive citizens. We go through hard and good times all together as a team. We never rest on our laurels–we challenge one another because that's how we continue to grow."

At their Web site, the Teen Tour Band keeps a list of what people have said about their band. In 1995, when the band was asked to represent the youth of Canada in Holland for the 50th anniversary celebration of Holland's liberation in World War II, former Prime Minister Brian Mulroney said:

Your achievement is an admirable one, and testifies to the strength of character of the young people of Canada generally and the citizens of the fine city of Burlington in particular. A community that can raise almost $3,000 to send its young musicians abroad as proud ambassadors of Canada must be a special place indeed, and my Government and I thank you sincerely. Through your musical goodwill, you have enhanced the reputation of all Canadians. I wish you all every good fortune in future endeavors, and I thank you again for making us proud to call Canada home."

Whether or not a marching band comes home with a trophy, there is an excitement in competing that cannot be beat. It takes a dedicated group of people to perfect making music and marching together. When everybody in the band is working together and enjoying the work, everyone is a winner.

Glossary

adjudicator – The judge for a marching band competition.

articulate – To play clearly and distinctly.

attack – The manner in which a note is played.

audition – A type of competition in which a band submits tapes of its performance and waits for a judge's decision.

balance – Making sure each instrument is equal in volume.

beat – The main rhythm in music.

blend – Making sure the tone qualities of different instruments match up.

block formation – The square or rectangular arrangement of a marching band on a field or in a parade

bore – A hollow tube that is the base of an instrument like a flute.

cadence – Marching steps that match the music's time and tempo.

caption – A judging category in a competition.

charts – Diagrams showing the drill formations for field marching.

closer – The final piece in a marching band's field performance.

color presentation – An optional part of a field performance when the band displays the national flag.

counter-melody – Secondary melody to the main melody.

drill – An exercise; drill is also a term used to refer to the formations in a marching band show.

drone – A bagpipe sounding a continuous note to accompany the melody.

drum corps – Brass and percussion bands that perform in parades and competitions.

dynamics – The different levels of sound volume in a show.

execution – The technique or style of playing and marching that is judged in a marching band competition.

formations – Patterns band members use to move or stand on a field or in a parade during a show.

free form drills – Non-geometric arrangements of a marching band in a parade or on a field.

harmony – The pleasing combination of notes played at the same time.

in concert/out of concert – Terms used for production numbers held between the opener and closer of a marching band show.

instrumentation – The instruments used to perform any piece of music.

intonation – The accuracy of pitch.

invitational – A competition in which bands are invited to participate.

maneuvers – A series of moves that marchers coordinate with their music.

melody – The main part of a piece of music.

metronome – A ticking device that marks time at a selected rate.

musicality – Term that refers to the tastefulness and accomplishment of a piece of music.

opener – The first song performed in a competition.

pit – The percussion line that marching bands sometimes place at the front of their formation.

precision – The quality of being exact and accurate.

projection – Term for how well a sound can be heard.

reel – Lively Scottish or Irish folk dance music.

release – The way a musician ends a musical note or phrase.

rhythm – A regular, repeated pattern of sound.

spats – Stylish shoe coverings that snap around the instep and ankle.

sustentation – Holding notes to their full value.

symmetrical drills – Formations in which similar patterns of band members form around a central point.

tempo – The speed of music.

tone – A musical sound with pitch and character.

transverse flute – A flute held sideways when played.

visual effects – All the details you see in a marching band show.

Internet Resources

http://www.bandfest.com/festivals.html
All American Music Festival, a marching band competition held annually in Orlando, Florida.

http://www.bands.org
Bands of America (BOA) holds events for more than 60,000 teens each year.

http://www3.sk.sympatico/ca
The Canadian Band Association (CBA) is a national organization supporting school and community bands in Canada.

http://www.dci.org/corps
Drum Corps International (DCI) sponsors worldwide competitions for drum and bugle corps.

http://website.lineone.net
The International Military Music Society (IMMS) supports youth brass, percussion, and pipe bands worldwide.

http://www.tob.org
The Tournament of Bands (TOB) is a competitive band organization open to any middle school, high school, college, or university band in the United States.

http://www.wamsb.org
The World Association of Marching Show Bands (WAMSB) is an international group dedicated to promoting marching show bands.

http://www.wgi.org
Winter Guard International (WGI) sponsors regional marching band competitions as well as U.S. and Canadian contests for color guard and indoor percussion.

Further Reading

Ardley, Neil. *Music, An Eyewitness Book.* New York: Dorling Kindersley Education, 1993.

Bailey, Wayne, and Thomas Caneva. *The Complete Marching Band Resource Manual.* Philadelphia: University of Pennsylvania Press, 1994.

Garty, Judy. *Techniques of Marching Bands.* Broomall, Pennsylvania: Mason Crest Publishers, 2003.

Holston, Kim R. *The Marching Band Handbook.* Jefferson, North Carolina: McFarland and Company, 1994.

Koscielniak, Bruce. *The Story of the Incredible Orchestra.* Boston: Houghton Mifflin, 2000.

Gerstein, Mordicai. *What Charlie Heard.* New York: Farrar, Straus and Giroux, 2001.

Index

JUDY GARTY has been writing stories since she was in elementary school. A writer of news and magazine features for many years, she contributed to two regional Wisconsin history books and to *Chicken Soup for the Kid's Soul.* Her children's books include *Jeffrey Bezos,* a biography of the man who founded Amazon.com, and a second book for this series called *Techniques of Marching Bands.* Sometimes Mrs. Garty teaches middle school, and she always enjoys cheering for a good marching band.